Expressions
Common Core

Dr. Karen C. Fuson

GRADE

4

Volume 2

This material is based upon work supported by the
National Science Foundation
under Grant Numbers
ESI-9816320, REC-9806020, and RED-935373.

Any opinions, findings, and conclusions, or recommendations expressed in this material
are those of the author and do not necessarily reflect the views of the National Science Foundation.

HOUGHTON MIFFLIN HARCOURT

Cover Credit: (Polar bear) ©imagebroker.net/SuperStock

Printed in the U.S.A.

ISBN: 978-0-547-82432-1

4 5 6 7 8 9 10   0982   21 20 19 18 17 16 15 14 13

4500413771   B C D E F G

Name _____ **Date** _____

Homework

Write each measurement in millimeters (mm). Round the
measurement to the nearest centimeter (cm).

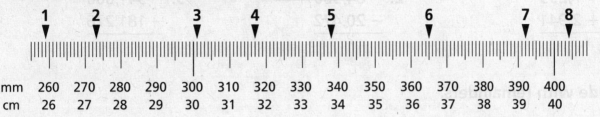

mm	260	270	280	290	300	310	320	330	340	350	360	370	380	390	400
cm	26	27	28	29	30	31	32	33	34	35	36	37	38	39	40

1. _____ mm rounds to _____ cm   2. _____ mm rounds to _____ cm

3. _____ mm rounds to _____ cm   4. _____ mm rounds to _____ cm

5. _____ mm rounds to _____ cm   6. _____ mm rounds to _____ cm

7. _____ mm rounds to _____ cm   8. _____ mm rounds to _____ cm

Write a number sentence to answer each question.

9. How many meters are equal to 7 kilometers?

_____

10. How many centimeters are equal to 4 meters?

_____

11. How many millimeters are equal to 15 centimeters?

_____

12. How many millimeters are equal to 12 meters?

_____

13. How many centimeters are equal to 2 kilometers?

_____

Solve.   *Show your work.*

14. Chester has a ribbon that is 2 meters long. He wants
    to cut it into 5 equal pieces. How many centimeters
    long will each piece be?

_____

Remembering

Add or subtract.

1. 7,295
    + 2,941

2. 84,366
    − 20,472

3. 541,000
    − 181,276

Divide with remainders.

4. $4\overline{)31}$

5. $6\overline{)44}$

6. $9\overline{)32}$

Evaluate.

7. $t = 5$

   $(9 + t) \div 2$

   _____

8. $k = 25$

   $k \div (10 \div 2)$

   _____

9. $p = 3$

   $(6 + p) \cdot (15 - 11)$

   _____

10. $g = 2$

    $(g \div 2) \cdot 8$

    _____

11. $r = 5$

    $(15 - r) \cdot (9 - 3)$

    _____

12. $x = 1$

    $(2 \cdot 8) \div (4 \div x)$

    _____

13. **Stretch Your Thinking** Kyle says the number is
    greater when an object is measured in centimeters
    than in millimeters. Is Kyle correct? Explain.

    _____

    _____

    _____

Homework

Complete.

1. How many milliliters are equal to 3 L?

_____

2. How many milliliters are equal to 35 L?

_____

3. How many grams are in 40 kg?

_____

4. How many grams are in 5,000 kg?

_____

Solve.

Show your work.

5. Every morning for breakfast, Mika drinks 20 cL of orange juice. How many milliliters of orange juice does she drink each day?

_____

6. Angie's puppy weighed 3 kg when she first got it. Two years later, it weighed 9 kg. How many grams did the puppy gain?

_____

7. Write and solve two word problems: one that involves converting units of liquid volume and one that involves converting units of mass.

_____

_____

_____

_____

Remembering

**Solve. Use the Place Value Sections Method and the
Expanded Notation Method for division.**

1. A coin candy machine contains 5,696 pieces of candy.
   With each quarter, a customer receives 8 pieces of
   candy. How many customers can use the candy machine
   before it must be refilled?

   $$8 \overline{)5{,}696}$$

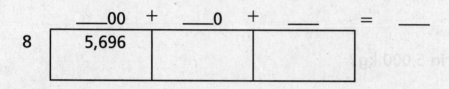

**Write an equation to solve the problem. Draw a model
if you need to.**

2. At the library one day, 1,742 books were checked out
   in the morning. Some more books were checked out
   in the afternoon. Altogether that day, 2,563 books
   were checked out. How many books were checked
   out of the library in the afternoon?

Write a number sentence to answer the question.

3. How many centimeters are equal to 6 meters?

4. **Stretch Your Thinking** Complete the double number line.

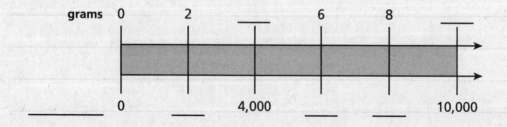

Metric Measures of Liquid Volume and Mass

Homework

Convert each measurement.

1. 45 min = _____ sec

2. 2 hr = _____ min

3. 3 years = _____ weeks

4. 1 day = _____ min

5. 6 weeks = _____ days

6. 18 days = _____ hours

Complete the line plot. Answer the questions using the line plot.

7. Melissa asked her classmates how much time they spend each day exercising. The table shows the data Melissa collected. Complete the line plot using the data from the table.

Time	Number
0 hour	0
$\frac{1}{4}$ hour	4
$\frac{1}{2}$ hour	3
$\frac{3}{4}$ hour	6
1 hour	2

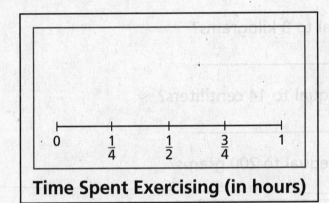

Time Spent Exercising (in hours)

a. How many more students exercised for $\frac{3}{4}$ hour than $\frac{1}{4}$ hour? _____

b. How many students did Melissa ask about how much time they exercise? _____

Solve.

8. Donald takes the bus to work. The bus ride is 37 minutes long. Donald gets on the bus at 7:22. At what time does Donald get off the bus?

_____

9. Kinesha started her homework at 6:15. She finished at 7:32. How long did it take Kinesha to do her homework?

Remembering

Solve. Use the Place Value Sections and the Expanded Notation Methods for division.

$5\overline{)1{,}895}$

1.

____00 + ____0 + ____ = ____

5	1,895		

Solve each equation.

2. $180 \div m = 3$

$m =$ _____

3. $r \times 9 = 108$

$r =$ _____

4. $350 \div 7 = p$

$p =$ _____

Complete.

5. How many grams are equal to 8 kilograms?

_____

6. How many milliliters are equal to 14 centiliters?

_____

7. How many milligrams are equal to 200 grams?

_____

Solve.   *Show your work.*

8. A full box of paperclips weighs 150 grams. People use some paperclips from the box, and it now weighs 138 grams. How many milligrams lighter is the box?

_____

9. Stretch Your Thinking Cassie and her family go to a restaurant for dinner. They leave their house at 5:25 and arrive at the restaurant at 5:53. They leave the restaurant at 7:09. How long does it take for the family to arrive at the restaurant? How many minutes pass from the time they leave their house to the time they leave the restaurant?

_____

Homework

Complete the tables.

1.

Yards	Inches
3	
6	
9	
12	

2.

Miles	Feet
2	
3	
4	
5	

Solve.

3. 4 ft = _____ in.

4. 3 miles = _____ yards

5. 11 yd = _____ ft

6. 26 ft = _____ in.

Write the measurement of the line segment to the nearest $\frac{1}{8}$ inch.

7.

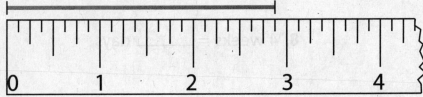

Solve.

8. Explain what is wrong with the ruler shown below.

_____

_____

_____

Remembering

Divide.

1. 6)582　　　　　　　　**2.** 5)4,961　　　　　　　　**3.** 7)6,334

Solve the comparison problem.

4. Michael made $265 taking care of his neighbors' pets
this summer. This was 5 times the amount he made last
summer. How much money did Michael make taking
care of pets last summer?

_____

Convert each measurement.

5. 9 days = _____ hrs　　　　　　**6.** 14 min = _____ sec

7. 6 hrs = _____ min　　　　　　**8.** 4 weeks = _____ days

9. Stretch Your Thinking Zack says that the line segment
is $3\frac{7}{10}$ inches long. Explain Zack's error. What is the
correct measurement of the line segment?

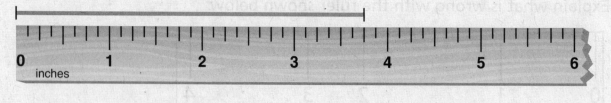

_____

_____

_____

Customary Measures of Length

Homework

Solve.

Show your work.

1. A female rabbit gave birth to 6 babies. Each baby weighed 4 ounces. How many ounces did the babies weigh in all?

   _____

2. One watermelon weighs 128 ounces. Another weighs 112 ounces. Which watermelon is heavier? By how many ounces?

   _____

3. A box of cereal weighs 21 ounces. Does it weigh more or less than 1 pound? How much more or less?

   _____

4. Mark had 3 quarts of milk. How many pints of milk did Mark have?

   _____

5. Trevon's mom bought 3 gallons of fruit juice at the store. How many fluid ounces of fruit juice did Trevon's mom buy?

   _____

6. Marinda made a drink that contained 2 pints of apple juice, 3 pints of grape juice, and 2 pints of cranberry juice. How many pints of juice did Marinda make?

   _____

Name _____ Date _____

Remembering

Solve using any method.

1. $7\overline{)643}$ 2. $2\overline{)5,698}$ 3. $4\overline{)8,913}$

Write and solve an equation to solve each problem. Draw comparison bars when needed.

Show your work.

4. Chris swam 94 laps at a pool for a fundraiser. This is twice the number of laps he expected he would be able to swim. How many laps was Chris expecting to swim?

_____

5. Jackie drank 60 ounces of water today, which was 12 more ounces than she drank yesterday. How much water did Jackie drink yesterday?

_____

Complete the tables.

6.

Feet	Inches
2	
4	
5	
8	

7.

Miles	Yards
3	
4	
8	
10	

8. **Stretch Your Thinking** Kai needs to pour 2 gallons of water into his fish tank. All he has is a measuring cup. How many cups of water should he put in the tank? Explain.

_____

_____

Customary Measures of Weight and Liquid Volume

Find the area and perimeter for rectangles with the lengths and widths shown.

1. $l = 5$ units   **2.** $l = 8$ units   **3.** $l = 7$ units   **4.** $l = 4$ units

$w = 6$ units $w = 4$ units $w = 5$ units $w = 7$ units

$A =$ _____ $A =$ _____ $A =$ _____ $A =$ _____

$P =$ _____ $P =$ _____ $P =$ _____ $P =$ _____

5. Challenge Using only whole numbers, make as many different rectangles as you can that have either the same area or the same perimeter as the rectangles in Exercises 1–4.

Solve each word problem. Show the formula you used to find the answer.

Show your work.

6. Enzo is building a dog run that measures 10 feet by 9 feet. How many feet of fencing does he need to fence in the area?

_____

7. A sheet of construction paper is 9 inches long and 11 inches wide. How many 1-inch squares of paper can Dwayne cut out of one sheet of paper?

_____

8. Mieko has a rug that is 6 feet long and 8 feet wide. Her room measures 9 feet each way. Will the rug fit in her room? How do you know?

_____

_____

_____

Remembering

Add or subtract.

1.   7,382
       − 2,990

2.   47,291
       − 3,845

3.   573,019
       + 32,485

Use an equation to solve.

4. A store pays $715 for a shipment of 38 board games to stock their shelves. Each board games sells for $24. How much profit does the store make on the sales of the board games?

Show your work.

_____

Solve.

5. A preschool uses 4 gallons of milk a day. How many fluid ounces of milk does the preschool use in a day?

_____

6. Stretch Your Thinking A bathroom has a length of 10 feet and a width of 9 feet. Kade wants to put down tiles on the floor that are each 1 square foot. Then he will put a baseboard along the edges where the walls meet the floor. How many tiles does Kade need? How much baseboard does he need? Show your work.

_____

_____

_____

_____

_____

Perimeter and Area of Rectangles

Homework

Name _____ **Date** _____

Solve.   *Show Your Work.*

1. Barbara has a rectangular shaped mouse pad. The longest side of the mouse pad is 8 inches and the shortest side is 3 inches. What is the perimeter and area of the mouse pad?

   _____

2. Yeasmin has a cup with 27 milliliters of milk in it. She pours another 34 milliliters of milk into the cup. She then drinks 14 milliliters of the milk. How much milk is left in the cup?

   _____

3. John's dog weighed 7 pounds when he got him. The dog's weight tripled each year for two years. How many ounces does John's dog now weigh?

   _____

4. The area of a rectangular shaped living room was 240 sq ft. The longest side of the room was 20 ft. What is the length of the small side of the room?

   _____

5. A grapefruit has a mass of 100 grams. A watermelon has a mass of 4 times the mass of the grapefruit. What is the mass of the watermelon, in centigrams?

   _____

6. Hannah ran 200 yards during recess. Juanita ran 340 yards during recess. In feet, how much further did Juanita run than Hannah?

   _____

7. The perimeter of the rectangular shaped building is 960 ft. The shortest side of the building is 150 ft. What is the length of one of the longest sides of the building?

   _____

Name _____ Date _____

Remembering

Solve by any method. Then check your answer by rounding and estimating.

1. $6\overline{)49}$ **2.** $4\overline{)502}$ **3.** $6\overline{)3{,}781}$

Use an equation to solve.

4. Sydney bakes mini muffins for a bake sale. She bakes 4 pans that hold 12 muffins each and 3 pans that hold 18 muffins each. How many muffins does Sydney bake?

_____

Find the area and perimeter for rectangles with the lengths and widths shown.

5. $l = 8$ units   **6.** $l = 2$ units   **7.** $l = 12$ units

    $w = 7$ units $w = 14$ units $w = 3$ units

    $A = $ _____ $A = $ _____ $A = $ _____

    $P = $ _____ $P = $ _____ $P = $ _____

8. Stretch Your Thinking Ms. Carpse writes the following problem on the board. *A 20-foot length of ribbon is cut into 4 equal pieces. How many inches long is each piece of ribbon?* Ashe says you should first divide 20 feet by 4, then convert to inches. Wesley says you should first convert 20 feet to inches, then divide by 4. Explain how both students are correct.

_____

_____

_____

_____

       Solve Measurement Problems

Homework

Solve.

Show Your Work.

1. Yonni has a 5 gallon fish tank. He needs to change the water in the fish tank. How many cups of water will Yonni need to replace all the water in the fish tank?

_____

2. Barry is building a fence around his backyard. The backyard is in the shape of a rectangle and the longest side of the yard is 20 meters. The fence will have a perimeter of 60 meters. How many meters long is the short side of the backyard?

_____

3. Yesi's dog weighed 5 pounds when she got him. He now weighs 45 pounds. How much weight did Yesi's dog gain, in ounces?

_____

4. Fiona's family is replacing the carpet in their living room. The living room is in the shape of a square. The length of one wall is 16 feet. How many square feet of carpet does Fiona's family need to buy to replace their old carpet?

_____

5. Trevon drew the two rectangles below. He wanted to know the difference between the areas of the two rectangles. What is the difference between the two areas?

16 dm

9 dm

12 dm

7 dm

_____

Remembering

Solve. Then explain the meaning of the remainder.

1. There are 43 students at a musical performance. Each row in the auditorium has 8 seats. If the students fill seats row by row from front to back, how many people are in the last row?

_____

_____

_____

Write whether each number is *prime* or *composite*.

2. 49

_____

3. 31

_____

4. 17

_____

Solve.

Show your work.

5. The perimeter of a postage stamp is 90 millimeters. The longer side of the stamp is 25 millimeters. What is the length of the shorter side?

_____

_____

6. **Stretch Your Thinking** The directions for lemonade say to put 2 cups of the liquid concentrate into 1 gallon of water. If Olivia only wants to make 1 pint of lemonade, how many fluid ounces of concentrate should she use? Explain.

_____

_____

_____

_____

_____

_____

_____

     Focus on Mathematical Practices

Name _____ **Date** _____

Homework

Write each fraction as a sum of unit fractions.

1. $\frac{2}{4} =$ _____

2. $\frac{5}{8} =$ _____

3. $\frac{2}{6} =$ _____

4. $\frac{7}{8} =$ _____

5. $\frac{4}{12} =$ _____

6. $\frac{6}{12} =$ _____

7. $\frac{8}{12} =$ _____

8. $\frac{4}{6} =$ _____

Name the fraction for each sum of unit fractions.

9. $\frac{1}{4} + \frac{1}{4} + \frac{1}{4} =$ _____

10. $\frac{1}{8} + \frac{1}{8} + \frac{1}{8} =$ _____

11. $\frac{1}{8} + \frac{1}{8} + \frac{1}{8} + \frac{1}{8} =$ _____

12. $\frac{1}{12} + \frac{1}{12} + \frac{1}{12} + \frac{1}{12} + \frac{1}{12} + \frac{1}{12} + \frac{1}{12} =$ _____

13. $\frac{1}{12} + \frac{1}{12} =$ _____

14. $\frac{1}{6} + \frac{1}{6} + \frac{1}{6} =$ _____

15. $\frac{1}{6} + \frac{1}{6} + \frac{1}{6} + \frac{1}{6} + \frac{1}{6} =$ _____

16. $\frac{1}{8} + \frac{1}{8} + \frac{1}{8} + \frac{1}{8} + \frac{1}{8} + \frac{1}{8} =$ _____

Write three things you learned today about fractions.

_____

_____

_____

_____

Name _____   Date _____

Remembering

Solve using any method and show your work.
Check your work with estimation.

1. 2×87

_____

2. 35×64

_____

3. $\begin{array}{r} 336 \\ \times\ \ 8 \\ \hline \end{array}$

Solve using any method.

4. $5\overline{)481}$

5. $4\overline{)2,575}$

6. $7\overline{)3,855}$

Simplify each expression.

7. $(7 - 3) \cdot 8 =$ _____

8. $(6 \cdot 3) \div (11 - 9) =$ _____

9. $9t - 3t =$ _____

10. $(12n - n) + 5n =$ _____

11. Stretch Your Thinking Kia has a long piece of ribbon.
She cuts the ribbon in half then cuts each of those
halves in half again. Draw the cut ribbon. Kia uses
3 of the cut pieces for wrapping bouquets of flowers.
Write a sum of unit fractions and the total to show
the amount of the ribbon she has used. What fraction
represents the amount she has left over?

_____

_____

_____

Understand Fractions

Name _____ **Date** _____

Homework

Name the fraction of the shape that is shaded and the
fraction of the shape that is not shaded. Then, write an
equation that shows how the two fractions make one whole.

1.

2.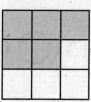

3.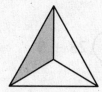

shaded: _____

unshaded: _____

equation: _____

shaded: _____

unshaded: _____

equation: _____

shaded: _____

unshaded: _____

equation: _____

Write the fraction that will complete each equation.

4. $1 = \frac{3}{3} = \frac{1}{3} +$ _____

5. $1 = \frac{8}{8} = \frac{3}{8} +$ _____

6. $1 = \frac{4}{4} = \frac{2}{4} +$ _____

7. $1 = \frac{10}{10} = \frac{7}{10} +$ _____

8. $1 = \frac{6}{6} = \frac{5}{6} +$ _____

9. $1 = \frac{9}{9} = \frac{8}{9} +$ _____

10. $1 = \frac{7}{7} = \frac{4}{7} +$ _____

11. $1 = \frac{12}{12} = \frac{9}{12} +$ _____

Solve.   _Show your work._

12. Kim drank $\frac{1}{3}$ of a carton of milk. Joan drank $\frac{1}{4}$ of a
carton of milk. Who drank more milk?

_____

_____

13. Maria read $\frac{1}{8}$ of a story. Darren read $\frac{1}{7}$ of the same
story. Who read less of the story?

_____

_____

Remembering

Write = or ≠ to make each statement true.

1. $25 + 25 \bigcirc 50$ **2.** $17 + 3 \bigcirc 30 - 10$ **3.** $9 + 8 \bigcirc 8 + 9$

4. $31 \bigcirc 23 + 9$ **5.** $3 + 1 + 12 \bigcirc 15$ **6.** $40 - 22 \bigcirc 18$

Solve each equation.

7. $8 \div b = 2$ **8.** $j \div 6 = 7$ **9.** $k = 5 \times 3$

     $b =$ _____ $j =$ _____ $k =$ _____

10. $q \times 10 = 90$ **11.** $12 \times r = 36$ **12.** $a = 7 \times 8$

     $q =$ _____ $r =$ _____ $a =$ _____

Write each fraction as a sum of unit fractions.

13. $\frac{4}{6} =$ _____

14. $\frac{6}{8} =$ _____

15. Stretch Your Thinking Margaret and June both made
a pumpkin pie of the same size. Each cut her pie
into equal pieces. Margaret's whole pie can be
represented by the fraction $\frac{8}{8}$. June's whole pie can
be represented by the fraction $\frac{6}{6}$. What is different
about the two pies? If Margaret and June each eat
1 piece of their own pie, who will eat more? Explain
how you know.

_____

_____

_____

_____

Solve.

1. $\frac{4}{8} + \frac{2}{8} =$ _____

2. $\frac{3}{11} + \frac{6}{11} =$ _____

3. $\frac{3}{4} - \frac{2}{4} =$ _____

4. $\frac{3}{5} + \frac{4}{5} =$ _____

5. $\frac{2}{6} + \frac{1}{6} =$ _____

6. $\frac{6}{7} - \frac{2}{7} =$ _____

7. $\frac{5}{12} + \frac{4}{12} =$ _____

8. $\frac{9}{10} - \frac{3}{10} =$ _____

9. $\frac{8}{9} - \frac{4}{9} =$ _____

Solve.   *Show your work.*

10. Sue is driving to see her mom. The first day she traveled $\frac{2}{5}$ of the distance. The next day she traveled another $\frac{2}{5}$ of the distance. What fraction of the distance has she driven?

_____

11. When Keshawn sharpens her pencil, she loses about $\frac{1}{12}$ of the length. One day, she sharpened her pencil 3 times. The next day she sharpened the same pencil 5 times. What fraction of the pencil did Keshawn sharpen away?

_____

12. One day, a flower shop sold $\frac{7}{10}$ of its roses in the morning and $\frac{2}{10}$ of its roses in the afternoon. What fraction of its roses did the shop sell that day?

_____

13. Bonnie's orange was cut into eighths. She ate $\frac{3}{8}$ of the orange and her friend ate $\frac{3}{8}$ of it. Did they eat the whole orange? Explain.

_____

14. Write and solve a fraction word problem of your own.

_____

_____

_____

Remembering

Solve the comparison problem.

1. There are 108 cars parked in front of a building. This is 4 times the number of cars that are parked in the back of the building. How many cars are parked in the back of the building?

_____

Write a number sentence to answer each question.

2. How many millimeters are equal to 8 meters?

_____

3. How many centimeters are equal to 35 kilometers?

_____

4. How many meters are equal to 72 kilometers?

_____

Name the fraction that will complete each equation.

5. $1 = \frac{6}{6} = \frac{4}{6} +$ _____

6. $1 = \frac{10}{10} = \frac{1}{10} +$ _____

7. $1 = \frac{3}{3} = \frac{2}{3} +$ _____

8. $1 = \frac{8}{8} = \frac{4}{8} +$ _____

9. **Stretch Your Thinking** Lilly started the morning with a glass of juice that was $\frac{4}{5}$ full. She drank $\frac{3}{5}$ of the glass, then partially refilled with another $\frac{2}{5}$ of a glass. At this point, how full is Lilly's glass with juice? Explain your answer.

_____

_____

Add and Subtract Fractions with Like Denominators

Homework

Write the equivalent fraction.

1. $6\frac{2}{5} =$ _____

2. $2\frac{3}{8} =$ _____

3. $4\frac{6}{7} =$ _____

4. $8\frac{1}{3} =$ _____

5. $3\frac{7}{10} =$ _____

6. $5\frac{5}{6} =$ _____

7. $7\frac{3}{4} =$ _____

8. $1\frac{4}{9} =$ _____

Write the equivalent mixed number.

9. $\frac{50}{7} =$ _____

10. $\frac{16}{10} =$ _____

11. $\frac{23}{4} =$ _____

12. $\frac{50}{5} =$ _____

13. $\frac{21}{8} =$ _____

14. $\frac{11}{3} =$ _____

15. $\frac{60}{9} =$ _____

16. $\frac{23}{5} =$ _____

Solve.

Show your work.

17. Castor brought $6\frac{3}{4}$ small carrot cakes to share with the 26 students in his class. Did Castor bring enough for each student to have $\frac{1}{4}$ of a cake? Explain your thinking.

_____

_____

18. Claire cut some apples into eighths. She and her friends ate all but 17 pieces. How many whole apples and parts of apples did she have left over? Tell how you know.

_____

_____

Name _____ **Date** _____

Remembering

Write and solve an equation to solve each problem.
Draw comparison bars when needed.

Show your work.

1. Brigitte fostered 14 dogs this year, which is 5 less than last year. How many dogs did Brigitte foster last year?

_____

2. Rema has two jobs. In one year, she worked 276 hours at her first job. In the same year, she worked 3 times the number of hours at her second job. How many hours did Rema work that year at her second job?

_____

Complete.

3. How many milliliters are equal to 21 L? _____

4. How many milligrams are equal to 9 g? _____

5. How many grams are equal to 400 kg? _____

Solve.

6. $\frac{3}{4} - \frac{1}{4} =$ _____

7. $\frac{2}{9} + \frac{3}{9} =$ _____

8. $\frac{7}{8} - \frac{1}{8} =$ _____

9. **Stretch Your Thinking** Harrison says that to convert a mixed number to a fraction greater than 1, he thinks of it this way: $4\frac{2}{5} = \frac{5}{5} + \frac{5}{5} + \frac{5}{5} + \frac{5}{5} + \frac{2}{5} = \frac{22}{5}$. Does his strategy work? Explain.

_____

_____

_____

_____

_____

Mixed Numbers and Fractions Greater Than 1

Homework

Add.

1. $3\frac{2}{6}$
$+ \ 6\frac{3}{6}$

2. $8\frac{5}{10}$
$+ \ 9\frac{6}{10}$

3. $7\frac{3}{4}$
$+ \ 4\frac{2}{4}$

4. $1\frac{5}{9}$
$+ \ 5\frac{7}{9}$

5. $3\frac{2}{5}$
$+ \ 3\frac{3}{5}$

6. $1\frac{2}{8}$
$+ \ 2\frac{5}{8}$

Subtract.

7. $7\frac{2}{3}$
$- \ 3\frac{1}{3}$

8. $8\frac{2}{7}$
$- \ 5\frac{5}{7}$

9. $6\frac{1}{4}$
$- \ 2\frac{3}{4}$

10. $9\frac{1}{8}$
$- \ 4\frac{5}{8}$

11. $9\frac{4}{6}$
$- \ 4\frac{1}{6}$

12. $3\frac{1}{5}$
$- \ 2\frac{3}{5}$

Add or subtract.

13. $\frac{1}{4} + \frac{7}{4} =$ _____

14. $\frac{3}{8} + \frac{6}{8} =$ _____

15. $\frac{9}{6} - \frac{8}{6} =$ _____

16. $\frac{5}{9} + \frac{6}{9} =$ _____

17. $\frac{9}{2} - \frac{6}{2} =$ _____

18. $\frac{5}{10} - \frac{2}{10} =$ _____

19. $\frac{2}{5} + \frac{4}{5} =$ _____

20. $\frac{8}{7} - \frac{3}{7} =$ _____

21. $\frac{7}{3} - \frac{2}{3} =$ _____

Add and Subtract Mixed Numbers with Like Denominators **137**

Name _____ **Date** _____

Remembering

The graph shows the number of miles Matt ran during a week of training for a marathon. Use the graph for Exercises 1–2.

1. On which day did Jason run 3 times the number of miles as he ran on Monday?

   _____

2. Write an addition equation and a subtraction equation that compares the number of miles Matt ran on Thursday (*x*) to the number of miles Jason ran on Tuesday (*y*).

   _____

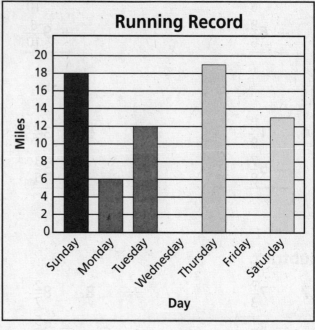

Running Record

Convert each measurement.

3. 4 min = _____ sec

4. 12 hrs = _____ min

5. 5 days = _____ hrs

6. 2 days = _____ min

Write the equivalent mixed number.

7. $\frac{9}{4}$ = _____

8. $\frac{12}{3}$ = _____

9. $\frac{63}{10}$ = _____

10. $\frac{11}{2}$ = _____

11. $\frac{14}{4}$ = _____

12. $\frac{15}{6}$ = _____

13. **Stretch Your Thinking** Garrett picked $12\frac{7}{8}$ pounds of peaches. Elise picked $13\frac{3}{8}$ pounds of peaches. Who picked more peaches? How much more? Explain.

   _____

   _____

   _____

   _____

Add and Subtract Mixed Numbers with Like Denominators

6-6
Homework

Write each mixed number as a fraction.

1. $6\frac{5}{8} =$ _____

2. $2\frac{1}{4} =$ _____

3. $8\frac{3}{10} =$ _____

4. $4\frac{2}{6} =$ _____

Write each fraction as a mixed number.

5. $\frac{26}{3} =$ _____

6. $\frac{47}{7} =$ _____

7. $\frac{59}{9} =$ _____

8. $\frac{44}{5} =$ _____

Add or subtract.

9. $\frac{2}{3} + \frac{2}{3} =$ _____

10. $\frac{5}{7} - \frac{3}{7} =$ _____

11. $1\frac{3}{9} + \frac{7}{9} =$ _____

12. $\frac{3}{4} + 3\frac{3}{4} =$ _____

13. $2\frac{4}{15} - \frac{10}{15} =$ _____

14. $\frac{15}{20} - \frac{6}{20} =$ _____

15. $3\frac{3}{5} - 3\frac{1}{5} =$ _____

16. $1\frac{1}{6} + 2\frac{2}{6} =$ _____

17. $2\frac{7}{8} - 1\frac{2}{8} =$ _____

Solve.   *Show your work.*

18. Rashid made a loaf of bread that called for $3\frac{1}{3}$ cups of flour. He combined white flour and whole wheat flour. If he used $1\frac{2}{3}$ cups of white flour, how much whole wheat flour did he use?

_____

19. Manuela spent $1\frac{3}{4}$ hours writing her book report. Katy spent $\frac{3}{4}$ hour more time on her book report than Manuela spent. How much time did Katy spend writing her report?

_____

Remembering

Add or subtract.

1. 23,546
   + 3,198

2. 50,427
   − 27,152

3. 850,000
   − 541,086

Use an equation to solve.

Show your work.

4. Each of Caroline's 2 older cats gets 7 ounces of food each day. Her younger cat gets 9 ounces of food each day. How much food does Caroline feed her cats altogether each day?

_____

5. Chad shares his 84 toy cars equally among his 3 friends and himself. Then he donates 15 cars to a used toy collection. How many cars does Chad have left?

_____

Add.

6. $3\frac{4}{9}$
   $+ 5\frac{2}{9}$

7. $7\frac{1}{5}$
   $+ 2\frac{2}{5}$

8. $9\frac{7}{10}$
   $+ 8\frac{4}{10}$

9. $5\frac{2}{7}$
   $+ 2\frac{6}{7}$

10. **Stretch Your Thinking** Chris ordered pizza for his family from a company that cuts its pizzas into 8 slices each. The fraction of a pizza eaten by each family member is shown in the table at the right. If they had less than 1 whole pizza left over, how many pizzas did they order? What fraction of a pizza was left over? Show your work.

Family member	Fraction of pizza eaten
Chris	$\frac{3}{8}$
Stacy	$\frac{2}{8}$
Rylan	$\frac{4}{8}$
Alec	$\frac{5}{8}$
Kelli	$\frac{3}{8}$

_____

_____

Practice with Fractions and Mixed Numbers

Homework

Multiply.

1. $3 \times \frac{1}{4} =$ _____

2. $5 \times \frac{1}{3} =$ _____

3. $4 \times \frac{1}{6} =$ _____

4. $7 \times \frac{1}{7} =$ _____

5. $2 \times \frac{1}{8} =$ _____

6. $3 \times \frac{1}{10} =$ _____

7. $2 \times \frac{3}{4} =$ _____

8. $12 \times \frac{2}{3} =$ _____

9. $12 \times \frac{5}{6} =$ _____

10. $3 \times \frac{2}{7} =$ _____

11. $24 \times \frac{5}{8} =$ _____

12. $8 \times \frac{3}{10} =$ _____

13. $20 \times \frac{3}{5} =$ _____

14. $9 \times \frac{5}{9} =$ _____

15. $10 \times \frac{7}{12} =$ _____

Solve.   *Show your work.*

16. Manuel eats $\frac{1}{8}$ of a melon for a snack each day.
    How much melon does he eat in five days?

    _____

17. Shannen collects paper for recycling. She collects
    $\frac{1}{3}$ pound of paper each week. How much
    paper will she collect in 4 weeks?

    _____

18. Aisha is unpacking boxes. It takes $\frac{3}{4}$ hour to unpack
    each box. How long will it take her to unpack 6 boxes?

    _____

19. Mrs. Suarez cut a pizza into 8 equal slices. Each
    person in her family ate 2 slices. If there are
    3 people in her family, what fraction of the pizza
    did they eat altogether?

    _____

20. Hailey is knitting a scarf. Each half hour, she adds
    $\frac{3}{7}$ inch to the scarf's length. How much length
    will she add to the scarf in 12 hours?

    _____

Name _____ **Date** _____

Remembering

Use an equation to solve.   *Show your work.*

1. Camille bought 2 pairs of pants for $29 each and a shirt for $18. She paid with $80. How much did she get in change?

   _____

2. On a weekend road trip, the Jensen family drove 210 miles on highways, where their car gets 35 miles for each gallon of gasoline, and 54 miles on city streets, where their car gets 18 miles for each gallon. How many gallons of gas did they use?

   _____

Complete the tables.

3.

Yards	Feet
2	
5	
8	
10	

4.

Feet	Inches
3	
4	
9	
12	

Add or subtract.

5. $\frac{9}{10} - \frac{3}{10} =$ _____

6. $\frac{2}{5} + \frac{4}{5} =$ _____

7. $2\frac{1}{8} + 5\frac{3}{8} =$ _____

8. $8\frac{6}{7} - 8\frac{2}{7} =$ _____

9. $4\frac{3}{6} + 1\frac{5}{6} =$ _____

10. $7\frac{1}{4} - 4\frac{3}{4} =$ _____

11. **Stretch Your Thinking** A worm moves forward $\frac{3}{8}$ inch every 5 minutes for 1 hour 25 minutes. How far does the worm move in this time? Explain.

   _____

Multiply a Fraction by a Whole Number

Name _____ **Date** _____

Homework

Draw a model for each problem. Then solve.

1. $4 \cdot \frac{1}{5} =$ _____

2. $7 \cdot \frac{1}{3} =$ _____

3. $2 \cdot \frac{3}{8} =$ _____

4. $5 \cdot \frac{3}{4} =$ _____

Multiply.

5. $12 \cdot \frac{5}{6} =$ _____

6. $9 \cdot \frac{1}{2} =$ _____

7. $25 \cdot \frac{3}{7} =$ _____

8. $12 \cdot \frac{4}{5} =$ _____

9. $5 \cdot \frac{2}{12} =$ _____

10. $9 \cdot \frac{2}{3} =$ _____

Write an equation. Then solve.

Show your work.

11. Cal's shoe is $\frac{3}{4}$ foot long. He used his shoe to measure his bedroom and found that it was 15 shoes long. What is the length of Cal's room in feet?

_____

12. The cafeteria at a summer camp gives each camper $\frac{2}{3}$ cup of juice for breakfast. This morning, 50 campers had juice for breakfast. How much juice did the cafeteria serve in all?

_____

Remembering

Solve each problem.

1. $24 \div 8 + 9 = h$

_____

2. $(14 \div 2) - (3 \times 2) = l$

_____

3. $20 - (5 \times 4) = p$

_____

4. $(2 \times 9) + 9 = g$

_____

5. $(3 + 7) \times (2 + 4) = m$

_____

6. $(9 \div 3) + (5 - 4) = t$

_____

Solve.

Show your work.

7. A baby weighs 7 pounds 2 ounces at birth. How many ounces does the baby weigh?

_____

8. Jack bought 2 quarts of motor oil. His car took 1 quart and another half quart. How many cups of oil does he have left?

_____

Multiply.

9. $6 \times \frac{1}{7} =$ _____

10. $5 \times \frac{3}{8} =$ _____

11. $2 \times \frac{9}{10} =$ _____

12. $8 \times \frac{3}{4} =$ _____

13. $3 \times \frac{1}{3} =$ _____

14. $15 \times \frac{3}{11} =$ _____

15. Stretch Your Thinking Write a word problem using the whole number 4 and the fraction $\frac{3}{8}$. Then solve your problem.

_____

_____

_____

Practice Multiplying a Fraction by a Whole Number

Homework

Add or subtract.

1. $\begin{array}{r} 2\frac{2}{3} \\ + 4\frac{1}{3} \\ \hline \end{array}$

2. $\begin{array}{r} 9\frac{7}{9} \\ - 4\frac{5}{9} \\ \hline \end{array}$

3. $\begin{array}{r} 5\frac{4}{5} \\ + 7\frac{3}{5} \\ \hline \end{array}$

4. $\begin{array}{r} 8 \\ - 1\frac{1}{6} \\ \hline \end{array}$

5. $\begin{array}{r} 18\frac{5}{8} \\ + 12\frac{7}{8} \\ \hline \end{array}$

6. $\begin{array}{r} 10\frac{1}{4} \\ - 3\frac{3}{4} \\ \hline \end{array}$

Multiply. Write your answer as a mixed number or a whole number, when possible.

7. $5 \cdot \frac{1}{5} =$ _____

8. $5 \cdot \frac{4}{7} =$ _____

9. $20 \cdot \frac{3}{10} =$ _____

10. $8 \cdot \frac{1}{6} =$ _____

11. $9 \cdot \frac{7}{12} =$ _____

12. $2 \cdot \frac{4}{9} =$ _____

Write an equation. Then solve.

Show your work.

13. At the science-club picnic $\frac{2}{3}$ cup of potato salad will be served to each student. If 20 students attend the picnic, how much potato salad will be needed?

_____

14. Skye spent $4\frac{2}{6}$ hours reading over the weekend. If she read $1\frac{5}{6}$ hours on Saturday, how long did she read on Sunday?

_____

Remembering

Tell whether 3 is a factor of each number. Write *yes* or *no*.

1. 12   **2.** 14   **3.** 38   **4.** 51

_____   _____   _____   _____

Tell whether each number is a multiple of 6. Write *yes* or *no*.

5. 46   **6.** 54   **7.** 21   **8.** 30

_____   _____   _____   _____

Find the area and perimeter for rectangles with the lengths and widths shown.

9. $l = 7$ units   **10.** $l = 2$ units   **11.** $l = 7$ units

    $w = 8$ units $w = 4$ units $w = 5$ units

$A =$ _____ $A =$ _____ $A =$ _____

$P =$ _____ $P =$ _____ $P =$ _____

Write an equation. Then solve.

Show your work.

12. Mattie walks $\frac{3}{4}$ mile to school and then back each day. How many miles does she walk to and from school in 5 days?

_____

13. A certain postage stamp is 2 inches long and $\frac{5}{6}$ inches wide. What is the area of the stamp?

_____

14. Stretch Your Thinking For a woodworking project, Tyler has cut 14 boards that are each $\frac{3}{4}$ yard and one board that is $2\frac{1}{4}$ yards. What is the total length of the boards Tyler has cut? Show your work.

_____

Homework

A pizza garden is a smaller version of a pizza farm. You can make a pizza garden at your home or in your community.

1. Use the circle below to draw a vegetarian pizza garden with 8 wedges. In each wedge, show one of the following vegetarian ingredients: wheat, fruit, vegetables, Italian herbs, and dairy cows. Use each type of ingredient at least once.

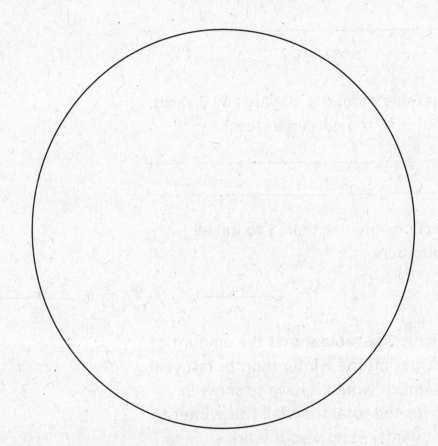

2. What fraction of your pizza garden is made up of wheat or fruit?

_____

3. What fraction of your pizza garden is *not* made up of vegetables?

_____

Remembering

Use the rule to find the next five terms in the pattern.

1. 7, 14, 28, 56, …

Rule: multiply by 2

_____

2. 10, 18, 26, 34, …

Rule: add 8

_____

Use the rule to find the first ten terms in the pattern.

3. First term: 3   Rule: multiply by 2

_____

Solve.

4. A rectangular vegetable garden is 10 yards by 7 yards. What is the perimeter of the garden in feet?

_____

_____

Multiply. Change fractions greater than 1 to mixed numbers or whole numbers.

5. $7 \cdot \frac{3}{5} =$ _____

6. $12 \cdot \frac{1}{2} =$ _____

7. $9 \cdot \frac{3}{10} =$ _____

8. Stretch Your Thinking The table shows the amount of snowfall, in inches, during the winter months last year and this year. How much would it have to snow in February this year for the total snowfall this winter to be the same as last winter? Show your work.

Last Year			This Year		
Dec.	Jan.	Feb.	Dec.	Jan.	Feb.
$12\frac{7}{8}$	$17\frac{1}{8}$	$26\frac{3}{8}$	$35\frac{5}{8}$	$11\frac{1}{8}$	?

_____

Focus on Mathematical Practices

Write > or < to make each statement true.

1. $\frac{1}{5}$ ◯ $\frac{1}{4}$

2. $\frac{6}{10}$ ◯ $\frac{5}{10}$

3. $\frac{4}{10}$ ◯ $\frac{4}{12}$

4. $\frac{3}{5}$ ◯ $\frac{4}{5}$

5. $\frac{3}{6}$ ◯ $\frac{3}{8}$

6. $\frac{7}{100}$ ◯ $\frac{8}{100}$

Solve. Explain your answers.

Show your work.

7. Juan took $\frac{2}{12}$ of the fruit salad and Harry took $\frac{3}{12}$ of the same salad. Who took more of the salad?

_____

_____

8. Kim drank $\frac{1}{3}$ of a carton of milk. Joan drank $\frac{1}{4}$ of a carton. Who drank more?

_____

_____

9. Maria read $\frac{3}{8}$ of a story. Darren read $\frac{3}{6}$ of the same story. Who read more of the story?

_____

_____

10. Write 2 things you learned today about comparing fractions.

_____

_____

11. Write and solve a fraction word problem of your own.

_____

_____

_____

Remembering

Divide.

1. $6\overline{)273}$

2. $2\overline{)1,935}$

3. $7\overline{)812}$

Write = or ≠ to make each statement true.

4. $16 - 4 \bigcirc 2$

5. $20 + 8 \bigcirc 30 - 2$

6. $9 - 4 \bigcirc 12$

7. $48 \bigcirc 24 + 24$

8. $50 + 3 + 8 \bigcirc 71$

9. $13 + 15 \bigcirc 15 + 13$

Solve each equation.

10. $18 \div s = 9$

    $s = $ _____

11. $m = 8 \times 4$

    $m = $ _____

12. $p \div 10 = 7$

    $p = $ _____

13. $t \times 12 = 60$

    $t = $ _____

14. $3 \times y = 18$

    $y = $ _____

15. $j = 42 \div 6$

    $j = $ _____

16. **Stretch Your Thinking** Ellen, Fern, and Kyle are all drinking milk from the same size cartons in the cafeteria. Ellen's carton is $\frac{3}{7}$ full. Fern's carton is $\frac{3}{10}$ full. Kevin's carton is $\frac{3}{4}$ full. Who has the least milk left in their carton? Explain how you know.

_____

_____

_____

_____

_____

Compare Fractions

Homework

1. Use the number line to compare the fractions or mixed numbers. Write > or < to make the statement true.

0   1   2   3   4   5

a. $\frac{3}{4}$ ◯ $\frac{5}{8}$ b. $1\frac{1}{4}$ ◯ $\frac{3}{2}$ c. $\frac{9}{4}$ ◯ $2\frac{1}{2}$ d. $\frac{7}{2}$ ◯ $\frac{17}{8}$

e. $4\frac{2}{4}$ ◯ $4\frac{5}{8}$ f. $4\frac{1}{2}$ ◯ $\frac{33}{8}$ g. $1\frac{3}{4}$ ◯ $1\frac{7}{8}$ h. $1\frac{1}{2}$ ◯ $1\frac{1}{8}$

2. Mark and label the letter of each fraction or mixed number on the number line.

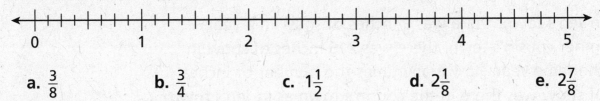

0   1   2   3   4   5

a. $\frac{3}{8}$ b. $\frac{3}{4}$ c. $1\frac{1}{2}$ d. $2\frac{1}{8}$ e. $2\frac{7}{8}$

f. $3\frac{1}{4}$ g. $3\frac{5}{8}$ h. $4\frac{2}{4}$ i. $4\frac{6}{8}$ j. $4\frac{7}{8}$

The list below shows the amount of fruit purchased from the market.

Fruit Purchases (lb = pounds)

apples $2\frac{1}{8}$ lb	bananas $2\frac{3}{8}$ lb
grapes $2\frac{2}{3}$ lb	oranges $3\frac{1}{10}$ lb

3. Decide if each weight is closer to 2 pounds, $2\frac{1}{2}$ pounds, or 3 pounds. Write *closer to 2 pounds, closer to $2\frac{1}{2}$ pounds,* or *closer to 3 pounds.*

a. apples _____

b. bananas _____

c. grapes _____

d. oranges _____

4. Which purchase had a greater weight?

a. apples or grapes _____

b. oranges or bananas _____

Remembering

Solve, using any method.

1. $8\overline{)1,219}$

2. $3\overline{)7,149}$

3. $4\overline{)4,038}$

Solve each comparison problem.

4. Mateo read 2,382 pages in a book series over the summer. This is 3 times the number of pages as his younger brother read over the summer. How many pages did Mateo's brother read over the summer?

_____

5. In Jen's town, there was 9 inches of snow in a year. In her cousin's town, there was 216 inches of snow in the same year. How many times the number of inches of snow was there in the cousin's town as in Jen's town?

_____

Write < or > to make each statement true.

6. $\frac{2}{5} \bigcirc \frac{4}{5}$

7. $\frac{1}{8} \bigcirc \frac{3}{8}$

8. $\frac{4}{5} \bigcirc \frac{4}{6}$

9. Stretch Your Thinking Dakota says the point on the number line shown here is $\frac{4}{5}$. His teacher says that he is reading the number line incorrectly. What is Dakota's error? What is the correct fraction?

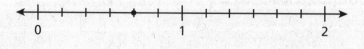

_____

_____

_____

Fractions on the Number Line

1. Draw a small square, a medium square, and a large square. Shade $\frac{1}{6}$ of each.

2. Draw a small circle, a medium circle, and a large circle. Shade $\frac{3}{4}$ of each.

3. Draw a short rectangle, a medium rectangle, and a long rectangle. Shade $\frac{3}{5}$ of each.

4. Look at the different size shapes you shaded in Problems 1–3. Describe what they show about fractions of different wholes.

_____

_____

_____

Solve.   *Show your work.*

5. Kris ate $\frac{3}{8}$ of a pizza and Kim ate $\frac{4}{8}$ of the same pizza. Did they eat the whole pizza? Explain.

_____

6. Amena ate $\frac{1}{2}$ of a sandwich. Lavonne ate $\frac{1}{2}$ of a different sandwich. Amena said they ate the same amount. Lavonne said Amena ate more. Could Lavonne be correct? Explain your thinking.

_____

_____

Remembering

Add or subtract.

1. 8,159
  + 2,713

2. 54,992
  + 8,317

3. 625,000
  − 139,256

Use an equation to solve.

4. Chad harvested 39 potatoes from his garden. He kept 11 for himself and shared the remaining potatoes evenly among his 4 neighbors. How many potatoes did each neighbor get?

_____

5. Mark and label the point for each fraction or mixed number with its letter.

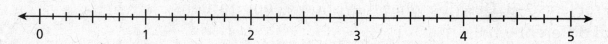

a. $3\frac{1}{8}$ **b.** $1\frac{2}{4}$ **c.** $\frac{3}{4}$ **d.** $4\frac{7}{8}$ **e.** $2\frac{1}{8}$

f. $\frac{5}{8}$ **g.** $2\frac{1}{4}$ **h.** $1\frac{3}{8}$ **i.** $3\frac{6}{8}$ **j.** $4\frac{1}{2}$

6. Stretch Your Thinking Raylene made a bracelet with 28 beads. She also made a necklace with twice the number of beads as the bracelet. If $\frac{1}{2}$ of the beads on the bracelet are green and $\frac{1}{4}$ of the beads on the necklace are green, does the bracelet, the necklace, or neither have more green beads? Explain.

_____

_____

_____

_____

Name _____ **Date** _____

Homework

Use the fraction strips to show how each pair is equivalent.

1. $\frac{1}{3}$ and $\frac{2}{6}$

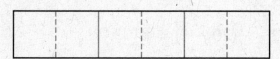

$$\frac{1}{3} = \frac{1 \times \boxed{}}{3 \times \boxed{}} = \frac{2}{6}$$

2. $\frac{3}{4}$ and $\frac{9}{12}$

$$\frac{3}{4} = \frac{3 \times \boxed{}}{4 \times \boxed{}} = \frac{9}{12}$$

3. $\frac{2}{5}$ and $\frac{4}{10}$

$$\frac{2}{5} = \frac{2 \times \boxed{}}{5 \times \boxed{}} = \frac{4}{10}$$

4. $\frac{2}{4}$ and $\frac{6}{12}$

$$\frac{2}{4} = \frac{2 \times \boxed{}}{4 \times \boxed{}} = \frac{6}{12}$$

Complete to show how the fractions are equivalent.

5. $\frac{5}{6}$ and $\frac{35}{42}$

$$\frac{5}{6} = \frac{5 \times \boxed{}}{6 \times \boxed{}} = \frac{35}{42}$$

6. $\frac{4}{10}$ and $\frac{40}{\boxed{}}$

$$\frac{4}{10} = \frac{4 \times 10}{10 \times \boxed{}} = \frac{\boxed{}}{\boxed{}}$$

Complete.

7. $\frac{4}{5} = \frac{4 \times \boxed{}}{5 \times \boxed{}} = \frac{\boxed{}}{45}$

8. $\frac{2}{5} = \frac{2 \times \boxed{}}{5 \times \boxed{}} = \frac{\boxed{}}{40}$

9. $\frac{3}{8} = \frac{3 \times \boxed{}}{8 \times \boxed{}} = \frac{18}{\boxed{}}$

Name _____ **Date** _____

Remembering

Solve. Then explain the meaning of the remainder.

1. Doris is putting together gift bags. _____
She has 53 favors to divide evenly _____
among gift bags for 7 guests. How _____
many favors will each guest get? _____

Solve each problem.

2. $2 \times 9 + 5 = r$ 3. $36 \div (20 - 8) = t$

_____   _____

Solve.

4. Mattie and Leah each bought an ice cream cone for the
same price. Mattie said it cost her $\frac{2}{3}$ of her allowance.
Leah said it cost her $\frac{1}{3}$ of her allowance. Who gets more
allowance? Explain.

_____

_____

_____

5. **Stretch Your Thinking** Omar cuts a pizza into 4 slices and
takes 3 of the slices. He says that he would have the
same amount of pizza if he cut the pizza into 8 slices and
takes 6 of the slices. Paul says he can cut the pizza into
16 slices and take 12 slices to have the same amount.
Who is correct? Explain.

_____

_____

_____

_____

_____

Equivalent Fractions Using Multiplication

Homework

Shade the fraction bar to show the fraction of items sold. Group the unit fractions to form an equivalent fraction in simplest form. Show your work numerically.

1. The manager of Fantasy Flowers made 8 bouquets of wild flowers. By noon, she sold 2 of the bouquets. What fraction did she sell?

$\frac{1}{8}$	$\frac{1}{8}$	$\frac{1}{8}$	$\frac{1}{8}$	$\frac{1}{8}$	$\frac{1}{8}$	$\frac{1}{8}$	$\frac{1}{8}$

Group size: _____   Fraction of bouquets sold: $\dfrac{2 \div}{8 \div}$ = _____

2. A car dealer had 12 red cars on his lot at the beginning of the month. The first week he sold 8 of them. What fraction did he sell that week?

$\frac{1}{12}$	$\frac{1}{12}$	$\frac{1}{12}$	$\frac{1}{12}$	$\frac{1}{12}$	$\frac{1}{12}$	$\frac{1}{12}$	$\frac{1}{12}$	$\frac{1}{12}$	$\frac{1}{12}$	$\frac{1}{12}$	$\frac{1}{12}$

Group size: _____   Fraction of red cars sold: $\dfrac{8 \div}{12 \div}$ = _____

3. A music store received 10 copies of a new CD. They sold 6 of them in the first hour. What fraction did the store sell in the first hour?

$\frac{1}{10}$	$\frac{1}{10}$	$\frac{1}{10}$	$\frac{1}{10}$	$\frac{1}{10}$	$\frac{1}{10}$	$\frac{1}{10}$	$\frac{1}{10}$	$\frac{1}{10}$	$\frac{1}{10}$

Group size: _____   Fraction of CDs sold: $\dfrac{6 \div}{10 \div}$ = _____

Simplify each fraction.

4. $\dfrac{8 \div}{10 \div}$ = _____   5. $\dfrac{6 \div}{12 \div}$ = _____

6. $\dfrac{25 \div}{100 \div}$ = _____   7. $\dfrac{4 \div}{8 \div}$ = _____

Remembering

Tell whether 4 is a factor of each number. Write *yes* or *no*.

1. 12

2. 20

3. 10

4. 26

_____

_____

_____

_____

Tell whether each number is a multiple of 3. Write *yes* or *no*.

5. 15

6. 32

7. 27

8. 25

_____

_____

_____

_____

Name the fraction for each sum of unit fractions.

9. $\frac{1}{8} + \frac{1}{8} + \frac{1}{8} + \frac{1}{8} + \frac{1}{8} =$ _____

10. $\frac{1}{12} + \frac{1}{12} + \frac{1}{12} + \frac{1}{12} + \frac{1}{12} + \frac{1}{12} =$ _____

11. $\frac{1}{9} + \frac{1}{9} + \frac{1}{9} + \frac{1}{9} + \frac{1}{9} + \frac{1}{9} + \frac{1}{9} =$ _____

Complete.

12. $\frac{3}{5} = \frac{3 \times \boxed{}}{5 \times \boxed{}} = \frac{21}{\boxed{}}$

13. $\frac{2}{9} = \frac{2 \times \boxed{}}{9 \times \boxed{}} = \frac{\boxed{}}{36}$

14. $\frac{5}{6} = \frac{5 \times \boxed{}}{6 \times \boxed{}} = \frac{15}{\boxed{}}$

15. Stretch Your Thinking Explain two different ways to simplify $\frac{6}{12}$.

_____

_____

_____

_____

Homework

1. Use the fraction strips to compare the fractions
$\frac{7}{12}$ and $\frac{2}{3}$.

$$\frac{7}{12} \bigcirc \frac{2}{3}$$

$\frac{1}{12}$	$\frac{1}{12}$	$\frac{1}{12}$	$\frac{1}{12}$	$\frac{1}{12}$	$\frac{1}{12}$	$\frac{1}{12}$	$\frac{1}{12}$	$\frac{1}{12}$	$\frac{1}{12}$	$\frac{1}{12}$	$\frac{1}{12}$

$\frac{1}{3}$	$\frac{1}{3}$	$\frac{1}{3}$

2. Use the number lines to compare the fractions
$\frac{5}{6}$ and $\frac{2}{3}$.

$$\frac{5}{6} \bigcirc \frac{2}{3}$$

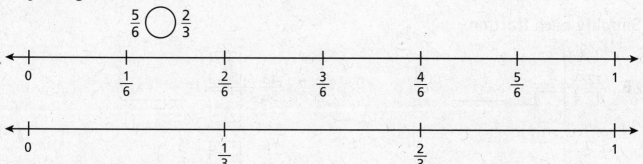

Compare. Write >, <, or =.

3. $\frac{1}{6} \bigcirc \frac{3}{5}$

4. $\frac{7}{8} \bigcirc \frac{3}{4}$

5. $\frac{1}{4} \bigcirc \frac{3}{10}$

6. $\frac{7}{10} \bigcirc \frac{5}{8}$

7. $\frac{2}{3} \bigcirc \frac{1}{2}$

8. $\frac{2}{5} \bigcirc \frac{7}{10}$

Remembering

Write a number sentence to answer each question.

1. How many meters are equal to 58 kilometers?

_____

2. How many millimeters are equal to 17 centimeters?

_____

Name the fraction that will complete each equation.

3. $1 = \dfrac{4}{4} = \dfrac{1}{4} +$ _____

4. $1 = \dfrac{8}{8} = \dfrac{2}{8} +$ _____

5. $1 = \dfrac{6}{6} = \dfrac{1}{6} +$ _____

Simplify each fraction.

6. $\dfrac{12 \div \boxed{}}{15 \div \boxed{}} =$ _____

7. $\dfrac{48 \div \boxed{}}{56 \div \boxed{}} =$ _____

8. $\dfrac{28 \div \boxed{}}{36 \div \boxed{}} =$ _____

9. $\dfrac{15 \div \boxed{}}{40 \div \boxed{}} =$ _____

10. Stretch Your Thinking Kathleen, Penny, and Megan all order 12-ounce smoothies. After 5 minutes, Kathleen still has $\dfrac{3}{4}$ left, Penny has $\dfrac{5}{6}$ left, and Megan has $\dfrac{5}{8}$ left. Who has the least amount of smoothie in their cup? Who has the greatest? Explain.

_____

_____

_____

_____

_____

_____

Compare Fractions with Unlike Denominators

Name _____ **Date** _____

Homework

Tyler asked his classmates the distance in miles from their home to the school. The distances they named are shown in the table.

Distance from Home to School (in miles)	Number of Students
$\frac{2}{8}$	5
$\frac{3}{8}$	3
$\frac{4}{8}$	4
$\frac{5}{8}$	5
$\frac{6}{8}$	3
$\frac{7}{8}$	7

1. Make a line plot of the data.

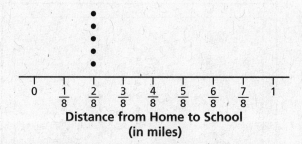

2. How many students did Tyler ask in all? Explain how you know.

_____

3. Find the difference between the greatest distance and the least distance.

_____

4. Layla lives the least distance from the school. Her friend Geneva lives $\frac{3}{8}$ mile from her. Geneva walked to Layla's house. Then the two girls walked to school together. How far did Geneva walk altogether?

_____

Remembering

Complete.

1. How many liters are equal to 39 kL? _____

2. How many milligrams are equal to 4 cg? _____

Solve.

3. $\frac{5}{9} + \frac{2}{9} =$ _____

4. $\frac{4}{6} - \frac{1}{6} =$ _____

5. $\frac{10}{11} - \frac{3}{11} =$ _____

Use a common denominator to compare the fractions.
Write <, =, or > to make a true statement.

6. $\frac{9}{10} \bigcirc \frac{2}{3}$

7. $\frac{5}{8} \bigcirc \frac{3}{5}$

8. $\frac{2}{3} \bigcirc \frac{5}{6}$

9. $\frac{4}{14} \bigcirc \frac{2}{7}$

10. $\frac{4}{5} \bigcirc \frac{4}{10}$

11. $\frac{6}{8} \bigcirc \frac{5}{6}$

12. **Stretch Your Thinking** Mr. Brady asked his students how long it took each of them to complete their homework from the previous night. He presented the results in the line plot shown. How many minutes did the greatest number of students take to do their homework? How many combined hours did those particular students spend on homework? Explain.

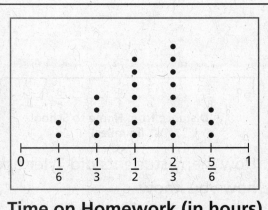

Time on Homework (in hours)

_____

_____

_____

_____

_____

Fractions and Line Plots

Use the visual to fill in each blank.

1. The shaded part of the whole represents:

$\frac{40}{100}$ = _____ of _____ equal parts and the decimal _____.

$\frac{4}{10}$ = _____ of _____ equal parts and the decimal _____.

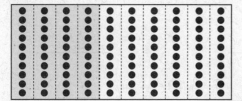

2. The shaded part of the whole represents:

$\frac{25}{100}$ = _____ of _____ equal parts, $\frac{1}{4}$ = _____ of _____ equal parts, and the decimal _____.

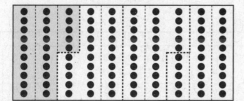

3. The shaded part of the whole represents:

$\frac{110}{100}$ = _____ of _____ equal parts, $\frac{11}{10}$ = _____ of _____ equal parts,

$1\frac{1}{10}$ = _____ whole and _____ of _____ equal parts, and the decimal _____.

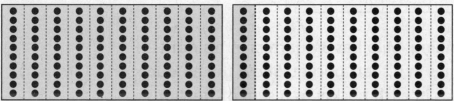

Solve.

4. Juan shaded a part of the whole. Four fractions represent the shaded part of the whole. List each fraction. Explain how each fraction relates to the shaded part of the whole.

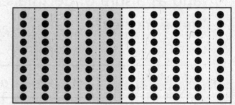

_____

_____

_____

Name _____   **Date** _____

Remembering

Convert each measurement.

1. 12 hrs = _____ min

2. 2 months = _____ wks

3. 43 min = _____ sec

4. 6 days = _____ hrs

Write the equivalent mixed number.

5. $\frac{12}{5}$ = _____

6. $\frac{19}{4}$ = _____

7. $\frac{15}{2}$ = _____

8. $\frac{29}{3}$ = _____

9. $\frac{49}{8}$ = _____

10. $\frac{37}{6}$ = _____

The line plot shows how much hair Emmy had cut each time she went to the hair dresser this year. Use the line plot to answer Exercises 11–12.

11. How many times did Emmy get her hair cut in the year?

_____

12. How much longer was the length of hair Emmy had cut most often than the length of hair she had cut least often?

_____

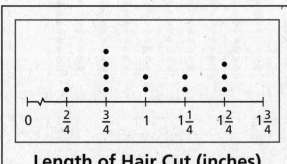

Length of Hair Cut (inches)

13. **Stretch Your Thinking** Milo has 3 quarters in his right pocket and 8 dimes in his left pocket. Show the amount of money Milo has in each pocket as a sum of fractions and as a sum of decimals. In which pocket is there more money?

_____

_____

_____

_____

Relate Fractions and Decimals

Name _____ **Date** _____

Homework

Write a fraction and a decimal number to show what part of each bar is shaded.

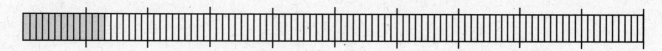

1. Fraction: _____   Decimal Number: _____

2. Fraction: _____   Decimal Number: _____

Write these amounts as decimal numbers.

3. 5 tenths _____   4. 9 hundredths _____   5. 56 hundredths _____

6. $\frac{80}{100}$ _____   7. $\frac{3}{10}$ _____   8. $\frac{1}{100}$ _____

9. 3 cents _____   10. 2 quarters _____   11. 3 nickels _____

Answer the questions below.

12. If you took a test with 10 questions and got 7 of them right, what decimal part would that be? _____ What decimal part did you get wrong? _____

13. If you had a dollar and spent 5 cents, what decimal amount did you spend? _____ What decimal amount do you have left? _____

14. If you had a bag of 100 beads and used 40, what decimal number did you use? Express this number in both tenths and hundredths. _____ _____

15. If you had to travel 100 miles and went 25 miles, what decimal part of the trip did you travel? _____ What decimal part of the trip do you still have left? _____

Name _____   **Date** _____

Remembering

Convert.

1. 7 ft = _____ in.

2. 4 mi = _____ yd

3. 15 yd = _____ ft

4. 2 yd = _____ in.

Add or subtract.

5. $8\frac{4}{8}$
$+2\frac{2}{8}$

6. $1\frac{1}{3}$
$+7\frac{1}{3}$

7. $5\frac{11}{12}$
$-1\frac{5}{12}$

8. $8\frac{2}{5}$
$-7\frac{4}{5}$

Use the visual to fill in each blank.

9. The shaded part of the whole represents:

$\frac{70}{100}$ represents _____ of _____ equal parts

and the decimal _____.

$\frac{7}{10}$ represents _____ of _____ equal parts

and the decimal _____.

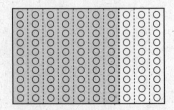

10. Stretch Your Thinking Rosemary put 7 dimes and
3 pennies in a tip jar at the café. Show this amount
as a decimal and as a fraction. How much more
change would Rosemary have to put in the tip jar
to make a whole dollar?

_____

_____

Explore Decimal Numbers

Homework

Write the decimal numbers that come next.

1. 0.05   0.06   0.07   _____ _____ _____ _____

2. 0.26   0.27   0.28   _____ _____ _____ _____

3. 0.3   0.4   0.5   _____ _____ _____ _____

Write each number in decimal form.

4. 9 tenths _____   **5.** 5 hundredths _____   **6.** 29 hundredths _____

7. $\frac{73}{100}$ _____   **8.** $\frac{2}{10}$ _____   **9.** $\frac{8}{100}$ _____

10. 4 pennies _____   **11.** 3 quarters _____   **12.** 6 dimes and 1 nickel _____

Solve.

A small jar contains 4 white gumballs and 6 red gumballs.

13. What decimal number shows which part of the gumballs are red? _____

14. What decimal number shows which part of the gumballs are white? _____

15. A large jar of 100 gumballs has the same fractions of red gumballs and white gumballs as the small jar. How many gumballs in the large jar are red? _____ How many are white? _____

A sidewalk has 100 squares. There are cracks in 9 of the squares.

16. What decimal number shows what part of the sidewalk is cracked? _____

17. What fraction shows what part of the sidewalk is cracked? _____

Write each decimal tenth as a decimal hundredth.

18. 0.6 = _____   **19.** 0.2 = _____   **20.** 0.5 = _____

Remembering

Solve. *Show your work.*

1. Mena bought a 1-gallon jug of water. How many 2-cup servings are in the jug?

_____

2. Kaden's filled backpack weighs 7 pounds. How many ounces does the backpack weigh?

_____

Add or subtract.

3. $\frac{7}{8} - \frac{3}{8} =$

4. $\frac{1}{4} + \frac{3}{4} =$

5. $10\frac{11}{12} - 5\frac{4}{12} =$

6. $\frac{2}{3} + \frac{2}{3} =$

7. $\frac{4}{9} + 3\frac{4}{9} =$

8. $8\frac{5}{6} - 4\frac{4}{6} =$

Write these amounts as decimal numbers.

9. 8 tenths _____

10. 5 hundredths _____

11. 27 hundredths _____

12. $\frac{2}{100}$ _____

13. $\frac{93}{100}$ _____

14. $\frac{7}{10}$ _____

15. 46 pennies _____

16. 3 nickels _____

17. 9 dimes _____

18. Stretch Your Thinking Ben says that 0.80 is greater than 0.8 because 80 is greater than 8. Explain his error.

_____

_____

_____

_____

_____

_____

Compare Decimals to Hundredths

Homework

Name _____ **Date** _____

Write each number in decimal form.

1. 6 tenths _____

2. 85 hundredths _____

3. 9 hundredths _____

4. 7 tenths _____

5. $\frac{4}{100}$ _____

6. $2\frac{9}{10}$ _____

7. $\frac{23}{10}$ _____

8. $11\frac{3}{100}$ _____

9. 6 cents _____

10. twelve *and* 5 tenths _____

11. thirty *and* 25 hundredths _____

Write each decimal in expanded form.

12. 27.9 _____

13. 153.76 _____

14. 203.06 _____

Use the graph to answer questions 15–17.

15. What decimal part of all the melons did Amy pick? _____

16. What decimal part of all the melons did Paco pick? _____

17. What decimal part of all the melons did Joey and Lisa pick together? _____

Melons Picked

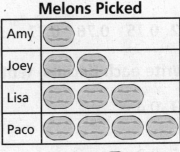

Key: ⬭ = 1 melon

Solve.

18. A centipede has 100 legs. What decimal part is one leg? _____

19. At a banquet, each cake was cut into 100 pieces. The guests ate 4 whole cakes and all but one piece of another. What decimal number represents the number of cakes that were eaten? _____

20. Miguel earned $10 and saved $3. What decimal part did he save? _____

21. Jing earned $100, and saved $30. What decimal part did she save? _____

Remembering

Add or subtract.

1. 5,000
    − 3,296
    _____

2. 286,361
    + 45,743
    _____

3. 863,542
    − 794,815
    _____

Multiply.

4. $4 \times \frac{1}{5} =$

5. $9 \times \frac{2}{3} =$

6. $3 \times \frac{7}{8} =$

7. $2 \times \frac{5}{12} =$

8. $5 \times \frac{6}{7} =$

9. $7 \times \frac{9}{10} =$

Write the decimal numbers that come next.

10. 0.03   0.04   0.05   _____   _____   _____   _____

11. 0.2   0.3   0.4   _____   _____   _____

12. 0.75   0.76   0.77   _____   _____   _____

Write each decimal tenth as a decimal hundredth.

13. $0.4 =$ _____

14. $0.9 =$ _____

15. $0.1 =$ _____

16. $0.3 =$ _____

17. $0.5 =$ _____

18. $0.7 =$ _____

19. **Stretch Your Thinking** A handful of paperclips is
    5.2 grams. A handful of push pins is 500 centigrams.
    Which handful weighs more? Explain.

    _____

    _____

    _____

Homework

Write these amounts as decimal numbers.

1. 4 tenths _____

2. 72 hundredths _____

3. 6 hundredths _____

4. 8 cents _____

5. $\frac{68}{100}$ _____

6. $9\frac{4}{10}$ _____

7. $\frac{16}{100}$ _____

8. $6\frac{7}{100}$ _____

9. 30 hundredths _____

Circle the number that does not have the same value as the others.

10. 0.95   0.950   0.905

11. 0.2   0.20   0.02

12. 0.730   0.703   0.73

13. 1.6   1.60   1.06

14. 0.59   5.90 $\frac{59}{100}$

15. 0.08   0.008   0.080

Write >, <, or = to compare these numbers.

16. 4.67 ◯ 12.7

17. 0.35 ◯ 0.4

18. 4.58 ◯ 1.25

19. 8.3 ◯ 0.83

20. 0.92 ◯ 0.91

21. 2.3 ◯ 0.84

22. 10.1 ◯ 10.01

23. 7.4 ◯ 0.74

The table shows how far four students jumped in the long jump contest. Use the table to answer the questions.

24. Whose jump was longest? _____

25. Whose jump was shortest? _____

26. Which two students jumped the same distance? _____

Long Jump Contest

Name	Length of Jump
Joshua	1.60 meters
Amanda	1.59 meters
Hester	1.7 meters
Miguel	1.6 meters

Remembering

Choose a measurement unit for each rectangle and find the area and perimeter. Show your work.

1. 11 by 8

_____

_____

2. 5 by 9

_____

_____

3. 2 by 6

_____

_____

Multiply.

4. $5 \cdot \frac{2}{3} =$ _____

5. $12 \cdot \frac{1}{5} =$ _____

6. $8 \cdot \frac{4}{7} =$ _____

7. $6 \cdot \frac{3}{8} =$ _____

Solve.

8. There are 10 servings in a bag of pretzels. At a school picnic, 3 whole bags are eaten and 7 servings of another bag. What decimal number represents the number of bags of pretzels that are eaten?

_____

9. Stretch Your Thinking Lance says that you can compare any decimal numbers the way that you alphabetize words. You can tell which number is less (or which word comes first in the dictionary) by comparing each digit (or letter) from left to right. Is Lance's thinking correct? Give a numerical example to explain your reasoning.

_____

_____

_____

_____

Homework

Write >, <, or = to compare these numbers.

1. $\frac{3}{4}$ ◯ $\frac{2}{8}$

2. $\frac{4}{10}$ ◯ $\frac{4}{5}$

3. $1\frac{3}{6}$ ◯ $2\frac{3}{6}$

4. $1\frac{1}{6}$ ◯ $1\frac{1}{4}$

5. $2\frac{7}{8}$ ◯ $2\frac{3}{7}$

6. $1\frac{4}{9}$ ◯ $1\frac{5}{10}$

Complete.

7. $\frac{3}{9} = \frac{3 \times \square}{9 \times \square} = \frac{\square}{45}$

8. $\frac{6}{10} = \frac{6 \times \square}{10 \times \square} = \frac{12}{\square}$

9. $\frac{5}{8} = \frac{5 \times \square}{8 \times \ 8} = \frac{\square}{\square}$

10. $\frac{24}{30} = \frac{24 \div \square}{30 \div \square} = \frac{\square}{5}$

11. $\frac{28}{35} = \frac{28 \div \square}{35 \div \ 7} = \frac{\square}{\square}$

12. $\frac{6}{18} = \frac{6 \div \square}{18 \div \square} = \frac{1}{\square}$

Solve.

Show your work

13. Cole lives 2.4 miles from the library. Gwen lives 2.04 miles from the library. Xander lives 2.40 miles from the library. Who lives closest to the library: Cole, Gwen, or Xander?

_____

14. After making his art project, Robbie has $\frac{2}{10}$ yard of rope left. What is $\frac{2}{10}$ written as a decimal?

_____

Remembering

Solve.   *Show your work.*

1. A 2-quart bottle of juice has 1,040 calories. Each serving is 1 cup. How many calories are in each serving of the juice?

_____

_____

2. The perimeter of a photograph is 20 inches. The longer side of the photograph is 6 inches. What is the length of the shorter side?

_____

Write an equation. Then solve.

3. Peggy needs $\frac{3}{4}$ cup of flour for each batch of pancakes. If she makes 5 batches of pancakes, how many cups of flour does she use?

_____

Compare. Use < or >.

4. 26.3 ◯ 8.3   5. 5.09 ◯ 5.9   6. 1.7 ◯ 7.1   7. 84.2 ◯ 8.42

8. 9.40 ◯ 9.04   9. 57 ◯ 5.7   10. 11.28 ◯ 12.8   11. 6.31 ◯ 6.13

12. **Stretch Your Thinking** On the first day of a trip, the Brenner family hikes 2.8 miles. On the second day, they hike $1\frac{2}{5}$ miles along a trail. They take a break, and hike back to where they started. Did they hike more the first day or the second day? Explain.

_____

_____

Focus on Mathematical Practices

Homework

Draw each geometric figure.

1. a point

2. a ray

3. an angle

4. Name the angle shown. _____

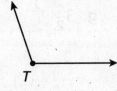

Look at the angles below.

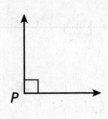

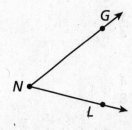

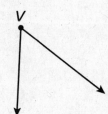

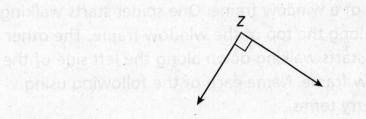

5. Which angles are right angles? _____

6. Which angles are acute angles? _____

7. Which angles are obtuse angles? _____

Remembering

Add or subtract.

1. $5\frac{4}{5}$
    $+ 3\frac{1}{5}$

2. $12\frac{5}{8}$
    $- 4\frac{3}{8}$

3. $3\frac{5}{7}$
    $+ 9\frac{3}{7}$

4. $6\frac{2}{9}$
    $- 2\frac{5}{9}$

Write < or > to make each statement true.

5. $\frac{3}{4}$ ◯ $\frac{1}{4}$

6. $\frac{5}{6}$ ◯ $\frac{5}{4}$

7. $\frac{7}{10}$ ◯ $\frac{7}{12}$

8. $\frac{6}{8}$ ◯ $\frac{4}{8}$

9. $\frac{4}{8}$ ◯ $\frac{4}{12}$

10. $\frac{17}{25}$ ◯ $\frac{21}{25}$

11. **Mark and label the point for each fraction or mixed number with its letter.**

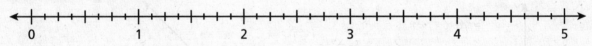

   0   1   2   3   4   5

a. $2\frac{1}{2}$

b. $3\frac{5}{8}$

c. $\frac{1}{4}$

d. $1\frac{4}{8}$

e. $3\frac{1}{8}$

f. $2\frac{3}{4}$

g. $3\frac{1}{2}$

h. $1\frac{7}{8}$

i. $\frac{6}{8}$

j. $4\frac{3}{8}$

12. **Stretch Your Thinking** Two spiders sit on the upper left corner of a window frame. One spider starts walking right along the top of the window frame. The other spider starts walking down along the left side of the window frame. Name each of the following using geometry terms.

a.) the place where the spiders began _____

b.) the walking path of each spider _____

c.) the type of angle formed by their paths _____

Homework

Use a protractor to find the measure of each angle.

1.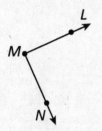

_____

2.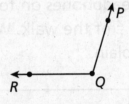

_____

3.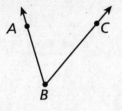

_____

4.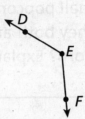

_____

Draw each angle.

5. an angle with measure 75°

6. an angle with measure 150°

7. On a protractor there are two scales. Read one scale to find 44°. What is the measure on the other scale?

_____

8. Which would be greater, the measure of a right angle or the measure of an obtuse angle?

_____

Remembering

Solve.   *Show your work.*

1. Presley ordered a small popcorn and Ella ordered a
   medium popcorn. They both ate $\frac{3}{4}$ of their popcorn.
   Who ate more popcorn? Explain.

   _____

   _____

2. It takes both Jack and Scott 12 minutes to walk to school.
   Jack had his headphones on for $\frac{2}{3}$ of the walk and Scott
   had his on for $\frac{2}{5}$ of the walk. Who had their headphones
   on longer? Explain.

   _____

   _____

   _____

Draw each geometric figure.

3. a line segment   4. a line   5. an angle

6. Name the angle shown.

   _____

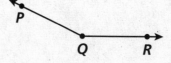

7. **Stretch Your Thinking** You can think of the two hands
   of a clock as rays of an angle. What type of angle do
   you see between the clock hands when the clock shows
   the following times? Draw a sketch, if you need to.

   a.) 3:05 _____

   b.) 6:00 _____

   c.) 9:10 _____

Homework

**Use a straightedge and a protractor to draw and shade
an angle of each type. Measure and label each angle.**

1. acute angle less than 40°

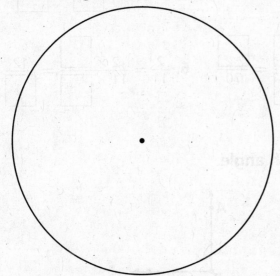

2. acute angle greater than 40°

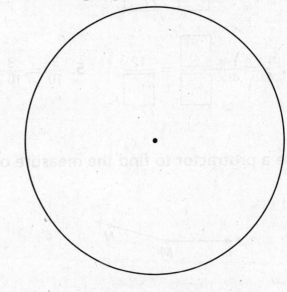

3. obtuse angle less than 160°

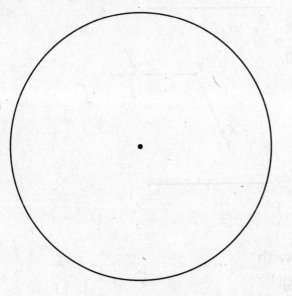

4. four angles with a sum of 360°

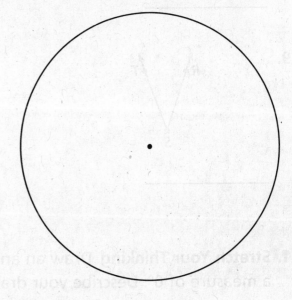

5. Write out the sum of your angle measures in
Exercise 4 to show that the sum equals 360°.

_____

Name _____ **Date** _____

Remembering

Complete.

1. $\dfrac{4}{7} = \dfrac{4 \times \boxed{}}{7 \times \boxed{}} = \dfrac{12}{\boxed{}}$

2. $\dfrac{5}{8} = \dfrac{5 \times \boxed{}}{8 \times \boxed{}} = \dfrac{\boxed{}}{40}$

3. $\dfrac{8}{9} = \dfrac{8 \times \boxed{}}{9 \times \boxed{}} = \dfrac{32}{\boxed{}}$

4. $\dfrac{1}{4} = \dfrac{1 \times \boxed{}}{4 \times \boxed{}} = \dfrac{12}{\boxed{}}$

5. $\dfrac{3}{10} = \dfrac{3 \times \boxed{}}{10 \times \boxed{}} = \dfrac{\boxed{}}{70}$

6. $\dfrac{2}{11} = \dfrac{2 \times \boxed{}}{11 \times \boxed{}} = \dfrac{12}{\boxed{}}$

Use a protractor to find the measure of each angle.

7.

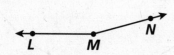

_____

8.

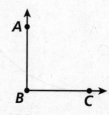

_____

9.

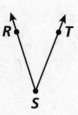

_____

10.

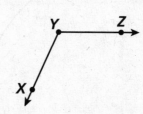

_____

11. **Stretch Your Thinking** Draw an angle with a measure of 0°. Describe your drawing.

_____

_____

_____

Circles and Angles

Homework

Name each triangle by its angles and then by its sides.

1.

_____

_____

2.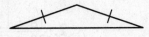

_____

_____

3.

_____

_____

4.

_____

_____

5.

_____

_____

6.

_____

_____

7.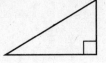

_____

_____

8.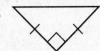

_____

_____

9.

_____

_____

10. Describe how acute, obtuse, and right triangles are different.

_____

_____

_____

11. Describe how scalene, isosceles, and equilateral triangles are different.

_____

_____

_____

Remembering

Simplify each fraction.

1. $\dfrac{9 \div \boxed{}}{12 \div \boxed{}} =$ 2. $\dfrac{18 \div \boxed{}}{30 \div \boxed{}} =$

3. $\dfrac{25 \div \boxed{}}{75 \div \boxed{}} =$ 4. $\dfrac{32 \div \boxed{}}{72 \div \boxed{}} =$

The measure of each shaded angle is given.
Write the measure of each angle that is not shaded.

5.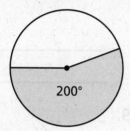

200°

_____

6.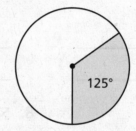

125°

_____

7. **Stretch Your Thinking** Aileen is trying to correctly classify a triangle by its angles. Her only information is that the triangle has at least one acute angle. Aileen says this must be an acute triangle. Is she right? Explain.

_____

_____

_____

_____

_____

_____

_____

Homework

Use a protractor to draw the two described angles next to each other. What is the measure of the larger angle they form when they are put together?

1. The measures of the two angles are 20° and 55°.

2. The measures of the two angles are 65° and 95°.

_____   _____

Write and solve an equation to find the unknown angle measure.

3.

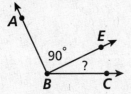

4.

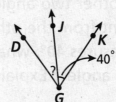

The measure of ∠ABC is 115°.

What is the measure of ∠EBC?

_____

_____

The measure of ∠DGK is 70°.

What is the measure of ∠DGJ?

_____

_____

5. When two 45° angles are put together, what kind of angle will they form?

_____

Remembering

Use a common denominator to compare the fractions.
Write >, <, or = to make a true statement.

1. $\dfrac{5}{8}$ ◯ $\dfrac{1}{2}$

2. $\dfrac{4}{6}$ ◯ $\dfrac{6}{9}$

3. $\dfrac{7}{12}$ ◯ $\dfrac{2}{3}$

4. $\dfrac{3}{10}$ ◯ $\dfrac{2}{7}$

5. $\dfrac{3}{4}$ ◯ $\dfrac{5}{6}$

6. $\dfrac{7}{12}$ ◯ $\dfrac{19}{24}$

Name each triangle by its angles and then by its sides.

7.

8.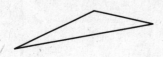

9.

_____   _____   _____

_____   _____   _____

10. **Stretch Your Thinking** Four angles are put together,
forming a straight angle. Two of the angles are the
same size. The other two angles are also the same
size but different from the other two. If one of the
four angles measures 40°, what are the measures of
the other three angles? Explain.

_____

_____

_____

_____

_____

_____

Compose and Decompose Angles

Name _____ **Date** _____

Homework

Write an equation to solve each problem.

1. Suppose you are bicycling along a straight road that suddenly starts sloping up a hill. You want to know what the angle measure of the slope is, but you can't measure inside the hill.

   If you are able to measure the angle on top of the road, however, you can use an equation to find the unknown measure. What is the angle of the slope of the hill shown?

   _____

2. On the clock face shown at the right, draw clock hands to show the times 3:00 and 5:00. One clock hand for each time will overlap with a clock hand from the other time. What is the difference between the measures of the angles formed by the hands of the clocks for the two times? (Hint: There are 30° between each pair of numbers on a clock.)

   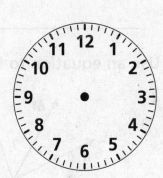

   _____

3. A lampshade is often sloped, with the top narrower than the bottom. For the lampshade shown, the whole angle shown is 122°. Find the measure of the unknown angle to find by how much the lampshade is sloped from upright.

   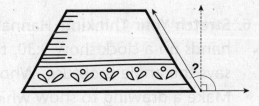

   _____

Remembering

The line plot shows the amount of cream put in a cup by each of a restaurant's lunch customers who ordered hot tea. Use the line plot for Problems 1–3.

1. How many customers ordered hot tea?

_____

2. How many customers used more than 1 tablespoon of cream?

_____

3. What is the difference between the greatest and least amount of cream the customers used?

_____

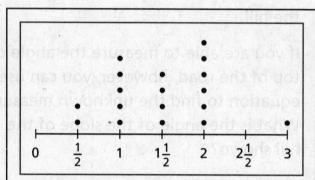

Cream in Tea (in Tablespoons)

Use an equation to find the unknown angle measure.

4.

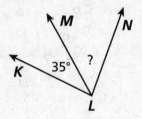

The measure of ∠KLN is 85°.

_____

5.

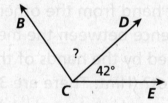

The measure of ∠BCE is 125°.

_____

6. Stretch Your Thinking Hannah says that when the hands on a clock show 9:30, the angle is 90°. Jennie says the angle is obtuse. Who is correct? Explain. Make a drawing to show which girl is correct.

_____

_____

_____

_____

_____

Homework

Which of the line segments below look parallel? Which look perpendicular? Which look neither parallel nor perpendicular? Explain your thinking.

1.   Parallel: _____ Perpendicular: _____

_____

2.   Parallel: _____ Perpendicular: _____

_____

3.   Parallel: _____ Perpendicular: _____

_____

Tell whether each pair of lines is parallel, perpendicular, or neither.

4. 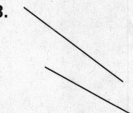   **5.** 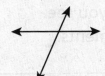   **6.**   **7.**

_____   _____   _____   _____

8. First draw a line segment 5 cm long. Then draw a line segment 7 cm long parallel to your first line segment.

Remembering

Use the visual to fill in each blank.

1. The shaded part of the whole represents:

   $\frac{30}{100}$ represents _____ of _____ equal parts

   and the decimal _____.

   $\frac{3}{10}$ represents _____ of _____ equal parts

   and the decimal _____.

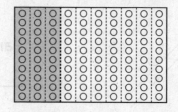

Write an equation to solve each problem.

2. A ladder leans up against a wall, as
   shown in the diagram. What angle
   measure does the ladder form
   with the wall?

   _____

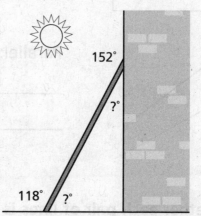

3. What angle measure does the ladder
   form with the ground?

   _____

4. **Stretch Your Thinking** Look around the room.
   Describe 3 pairs of parallel line segments you see.
   Describe 3 pairs of perpendicular line segments.

   _____

   _____

   _____

   _____

   _____

   _____

   _____

Homework

Using the Vocabulary box at the right, write the name of the quadrilateral that best describes each figure. Use each word once. Describe how it is different from other quadrilaterals.

1.

_____

_____

_____

2.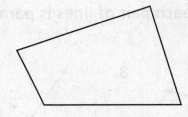

_____

_____

_____

3.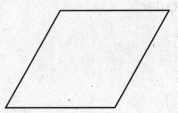

_____

_____

_____

4.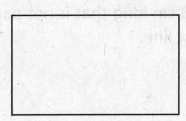

_____

_____

_____

5.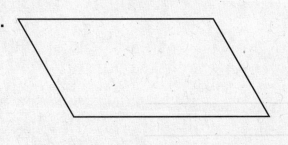

_____

_____

_____

6.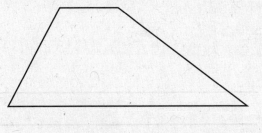

_____

_____

_____

Remembering

Write these amounts as decimal numbers.

1. 3 tenths _____

2. 7 hundredths _____

3. 56 hundredths _____

4. $\frac{6}{100}$ _____

5. $\frac{42}{100}$ _____

6. $\frac{9}{10}$ _____

Tell whether each pair of lines is parallel, perpendicular, or neither.

7.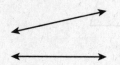

8.

9.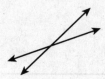

10.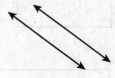

_____ _____ _____ _____

11. First draw a line segment 4 cm long. Then draw a line segment 3 cm long that is not parallel nor perpendicular to the first line.

12. Stretch Your Thinking Bianca has a certain shape in mind. She says it has all the following names: quadrilateral, parallelogram, and rectangle. Make a drawing that could be Bianca's shape. Explain why it has each of these names.

_____

_____

_____

_____

Classifying Quadrilaterals

Homework

1. Draw a rectangle and a parallelogram. Draw one diagonal
   on each figure. Name the kinds of triangles you made.

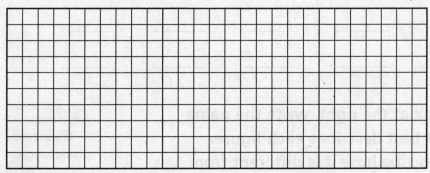

_____

_____

2. Draw your figures again. Draw the other diagonal
   and name the kinds of triangles you made this time.

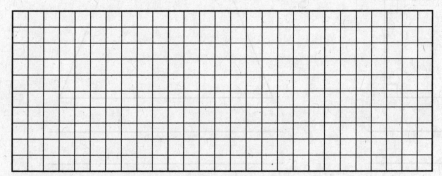

_____

_____

3. Use geometry words to describe how diagonals of
   quadrilaterals make triangles.

   _____

   _____

   _____

   _____

4. Use geometry words to describe a way to separate
   triangles into other triangles.

   _____

   _____

   _____

Name _____ **Date** _____

Remembering

Write the decimal numbers that come next.

1. 0.01   0.02   0.03   _____ _____ _____ _____

2. 0.3   0.4   0.5   _____ _____ _____ _____

3. 0.46   0.47   0.48   _____ _____ _____ _____

Using the Vocabulary box at the right, write the name of the quadrilateral that best describes each figure. Use each word once. Describe how it is different from other quadrilaterals.

VOCABULARY
trapezoid
rectangle

4.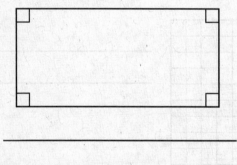

_____

_____

_____

5.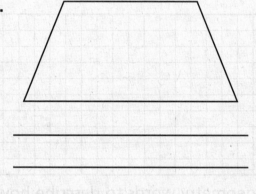

_____

_____

6. **Stretch Your Thinking** Suppose you drew a diagonal in each of the following quadrilaterals: rectangle, trapezoid, parallelogram. In which figures do triangles with the same size and shape form? In which figures do triangles with a different size and shape form? Explain.

_____

_____

_____

_____

_____

Decompose Quadrilaterals and Triangles

Homework

1. What are some different ways you could sort
   these three figures? Which figures would be
   in the group for each sorting rule?

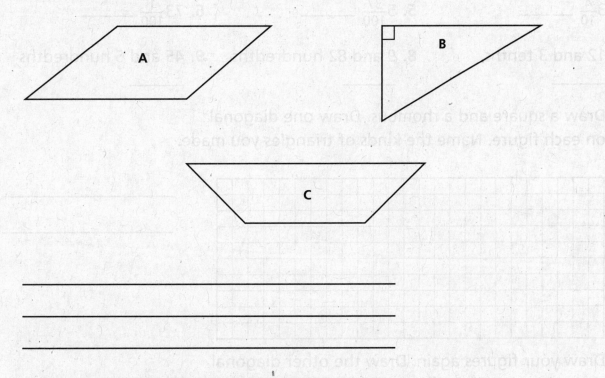

2. Draw a fourth figure to add to the figures in
   Exercise 1. Does it match any of the sorting
   rules you listed for Exercise 1?

Remembering

Write each amount in decimal form.

1. 8 tenths _____

2. 62 hundredths _____

3. 8 hundredths _____

4. $3\frac{4}{10}$ _____

5. $5\frac{37}{100}$ _____

6. $73\frac{1}{100}$ _____

7. 12 and 3 tenths

_____

8. 9 and 82 hundredths

_____

9. 45 and 6 hundredths

_____

10. Draw a square and a rhombus. Draw one diagonal
on each figure. Name the kinds of triangles you made.

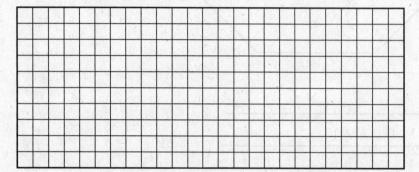

_____

_____

11. Draw your figures again. Draw the other diagonal
and name the kinds of triangles you made this time.

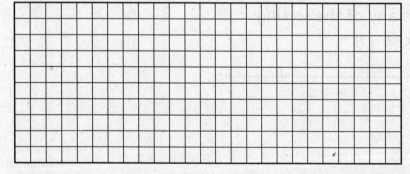

_____

_____

12. Stretch Your Thinking Draw and name three polygons
that each have at least one right angle. Label each right
angle on the polygons.

_____

_____

Classify Polygons

Homework

Name _____   **Date** _____

Tell whether the dotted line is a line of symmetry.

1.

_____

2.

_____

3.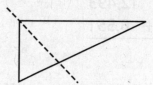

_____

How many lines of symmetry does each figure have?

4.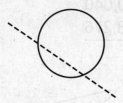

_____

5.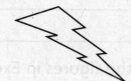

_____

6.

_____

7. Draw any lines of symmetry for this figure.

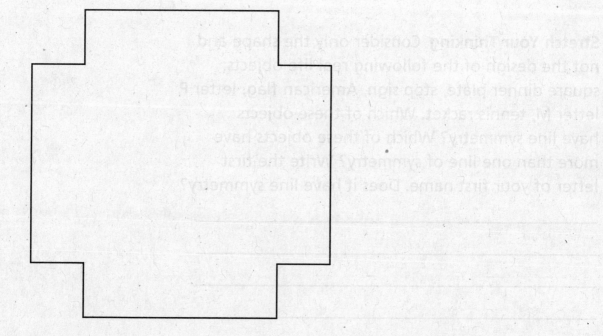

Remembering

Add or subtract.

1.   12,493
   + 6,551

2.   536,784
   − 69,205

3.   900,040
   − 318,276

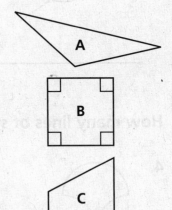

4. What are some different ways you could sort these three figures? Which figures would be in the group for each sorting rule?

   _____

   _____

   _____

5. Draw a fourth figure to add to the figures in Exercise 4. Does it match any of the sorting rules you listed for Exercise 4?

6. **Stretch Your Thinking** Consider only the shape and not the design of the following real life objects: square dinner plate, stop sign, American flag, letter P, letter M, tennis racket. Which of these objects have line symmetry? Which of these objects have more than one line of symmetry? Write the first letter of your first name. Does it have line symmetry?

   _____

   _____

   _____

Line Symmetry

Draw a flag design. The design must include a
quadrilateral with 2 lines of symmetry. The flag
must also have a triangle with a 45° angle.

1. What type of quadrilateral did you draw? How did
you make sure that the quadrilateral has 2 lines
of symmetry?

_____

_____

2. What type of triangle did you draw in the flag design?
What tool did you use to make sure that the angle
you drew measures 45°?

_____

_____

Name _____   Date _____

Remembering

Insert < or > to make a true statement.

1. 7.24 ◯ 72.4   **2.** 8.07 ◯ 8.7   **3.** 5.32 ◯ 3.52   **4.** 20.8 ◯ 2.08

5. 12.3 ◯ 3.12   **6.** 2.9 ◯ 29   **7.** 23.15 ◯ 24.1   **8.** 90.2 ◯ 9.02

Tell whether the dotted line is a line of symmetry.

9. 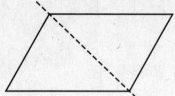   **10.** 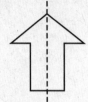   **11.**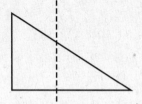

_____   _____   _____

How many lines of symmetry does each figure have?

12.    **13.** 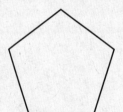   **14.**

_____

15. Stretch Your Thinking Design a pennant for your
school in the shape of an acute isosceles triangle.
Within the design, include a quadrilateral with four
right angles and at least one set of parallel lines.

_____

Focus on Mathematical Practices